MEL BAY'S

# THEORY & HARMONY
## for Everyone

by L. DEAN BYE

A **Workbook** of
the Fundamentals of Music

1 2 3 4 5 6 7 8 9 0

# FOREWORD

This book of basic music fundamentals is designed to be used by itself, or as a supplement to any traditional instrumental or vocal method. It has been written to provide those who are interested in becoming better musicians a basic knowledge and understanding of the elements of music; and may be used for private study or in a classroom situation.

To achieve the optimum end result, the student should engage in frequent and continued study, as well as intense additional drill and practice. All of this is aimed at the ultimate goal. That, of course, is to be a better and more knowledgeable performer, composer, or musical consumer.

# ABOUT THE AUTHOR

L. Dean Bye is a music educator, performer, and director. He is proficient on a number of instruments and has numerous years of teaching experience in the field of vocal music, as well as in theory, harmony, and music history.

# TABLE OF CONTENTS

| | Page |
|---|---|
| Foreword | 2 |
| Musical Notation and Pitch | 4 |
| (Musical Notation and Pitch -- Review) | 9 |
| Duration of Notes and Rests - Meter | 10 |
| (Duration of Notes and Rests-Meter -- Review) | 19 |
| Key Signatures - Major and Minor Scales | 20 |
| (Key Signatures - Major and Minor Scales - Review) | 28 |
| Form and Expression Marks | 30 |
| (Form and Expression Marks -- Review) | 33 |
| Intervals and Two - Part Harmony | 34 |
| (Intervals and Two - Part Harmony -- Review) | 38 |
| Transposition | 40 |
| (Transposition -- Review) | 44 |
| Triads (Tonic and Dominant) | 45 |
| (Triads - Tonic and Dominant -- Review) | 47 |
| Triads (minor and Subdominant) | 48 |
| Augmented and Diminished Triads | 50 |
| Dominant Seventh Chords (and Inversions) | 51 |
| Minor Seventh and Dominant Ninth Chords | 52 |
| Diminished Seventh and Augmented Fifth Chords | 53 |
| Chord Progressions and Passing Tones | 54 |
| Final Review | 55 |
| Charts -- | |
| Chromatic Fingering Chart For Guitar | 57 |
| Definitions of Common Musical Terms | 58 |
| Complete Chord Chart | 62 |
| Practical Ranges For Instruments | 64 |
| Theory Worksheets (Manuscript Paper) | 66 |

# MUSICAL NOTATION AND PITCH

THE STAFF: Music is written on a STAFF consisting of FIVE LINES and FOUR SPACES. The lines and spaces are numbered upward as shown:

| | |
|---|---|
| 5TH LINE | |
| 4TH LINE | 4TH SPACE |
| 3RD LINE | 3RD SPACE |
| 2ND LINE | 2ND SPACE |
| 1ST LINE | 1ST SPACE |

THE CLEF determines the letter names of the lines and spaces.

The LINES in the Treble Clef are named as follows:

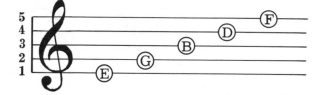

The letters may easily be remembered by the sentence - <u>E</u>very <u>G</u>ood <u>B</u>oy <u>D</u>oes <u>F</u>ine

The letter-names of the SPACES in the Treble Clef are:

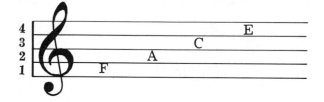

They spell the word F-A-C-E

As we can see, the second line of the treble clef is known as the "G" line. Many people call the treble clef the G clef because it circles around the "G" line. All other letter names are figured from this line.

On the following staff, practice writing the "G" or Treble Clef sign.

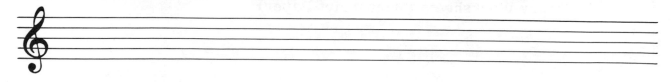

The Lines in the Bass Clef are named as follows:

These letters may easily be remembered
by the sentence -

Good     Boys     Do     Fine     Always

The letter-names of the spaces in the Bass Clef are:

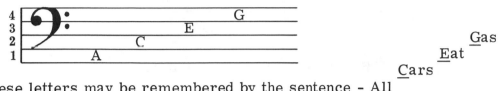

These letters may be remembered by the sentence - All     Cars     Eat     Gas

As we can see, the fourth line of the bass clef is known as the "F" line. Many people call the bass clef the F clef because the two dots are placed on either side of the line. All other letter names are figured from this line.

On the following staff, practice writing the "F" or Bass Clef sign.

Leger lines are short lines placed above and below the staff. Some examples are:

5

When both the treble and bass clefs are combined with an intervening leger line (middle C) it is known as the grand staff.

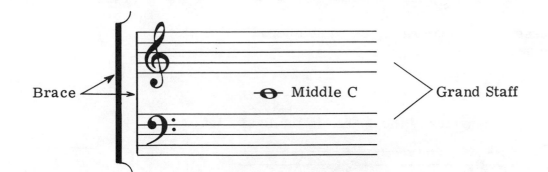

The perpendicular line and the bracket that joins two or more different staves is called a brace.

Under the following notes write the letter name of the note.

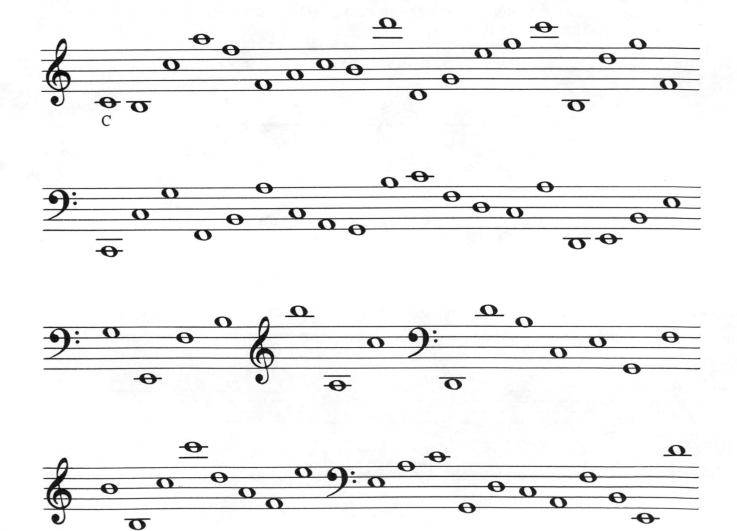

# STAFF NOTATION AND KEYBOARD POSITION:

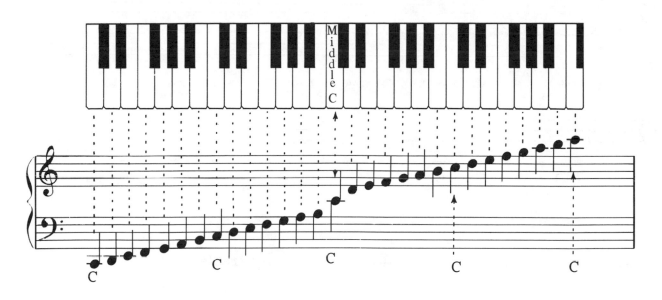

# STAFF NOTATION AND GUITAR POSITION:

The six open strings of the guitar will be of the same pitch as the six notes shown in the illustration of the piano keyboard. Note that five of the strings are below the middle C of the piano keyboard.

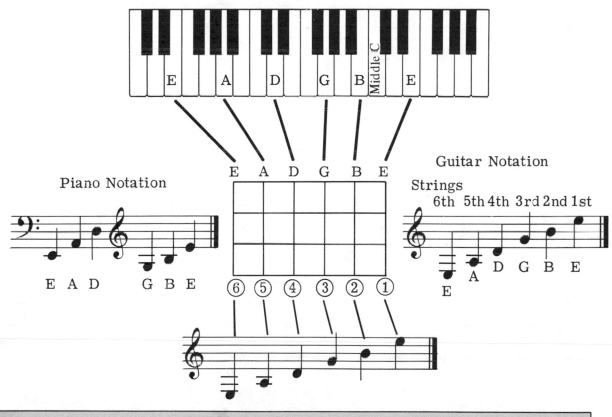

REMINDER: The Clef sign determines the letter names of the lines and spaces.

On the following Treble and Bass Clefs write the notes indicated.

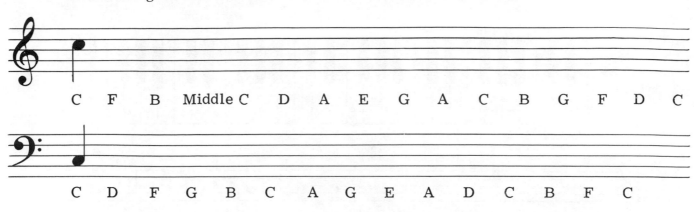

C　F　B　Middle C　D　A　E　G　A　C　B　G　F　D　C

C　D　F　G　B　C　A　G　E　A　D　C　B　F　C

Write the following notes one octave higher, on the treble staff:

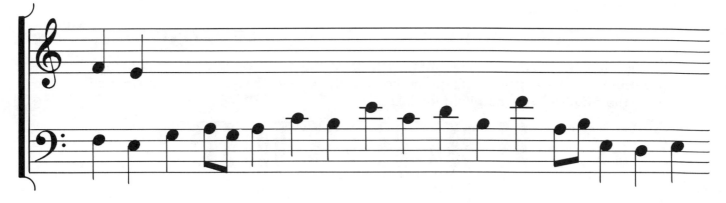

Write the following notes one octave lower, on the bass staff:

Drill in the letter names of notes and review of the staff location should be continued until the desired level of proficiency is attained.

# MUSICAL NOTATION AND PITCH
## (REVIEW)

1. The musical staff consists of _____ lines and _____ spaces.
2. Draw a treble clef and label the lines and spaces on the following staff.

3. Draw a bass clef and label the lines and spaces on the following staff.

4. The _____ staff consists of the _____ and _____ clefs along with middle C.

5. The _____ _____ determines the letter names of the lines and spaces.

6. Write the letter names under the following notes.

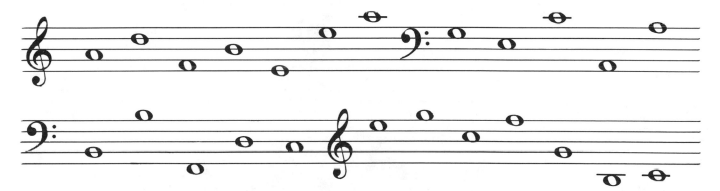

7. Write the notes above the proper letter.

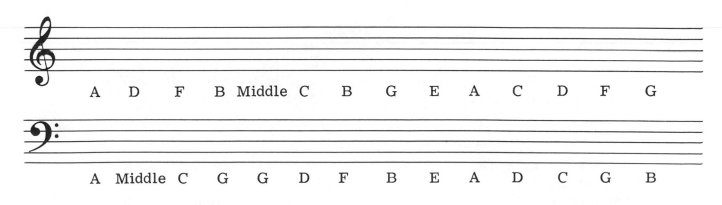

A   D   F   B  Middle C   B   G   E   A   C   D   F   G

A  Middle C  G   G   D   F   B   E   A   D   C   G   B

# DURATION OF NOTES AND RESTS --METER

TONE:

Music is composed of sounds pleasant to the ear.

SOUND may be made from NOISE or TONE.

NOISE is made by irregular vibrations such as would be caused by striking a table with a hammer, the shot of a gun, or slapping two stones together.

TONE is produced by regular vibrations as would be caused by drawing a bow over the strings of a violin, striking the strings of a guitar, or blowing through a wind instrument, such as a trumpet.

A TONE has four characteristics . . . PITCH, DURATION, DYNAMICS and TIMBRE.

PITCH: The highness or lowness of a tone.

DURATION: The length of a tone.

DYNAMICS The force or power of a tone. (Loudness or softness).

TIMBRE: Quality of the tone.

A NOTE represents the PITCH AND DURATION of a tone.

NOTES:

This is a note:

A note has three parts. They are — The HEAD

— The STEM

— The FLAG

Notes may be placed in the staff;     Above the staff;

And below the staff.

A note will bear the name of the line or space it occupies on the staff.
The location of a note in, above or below the staff will indicate the Pitch.
PITCH: the height or depth of a tone.     TONE: a musical sound.

TYPES OF NOTES: The type of note will indicate the length of its sound.

This is a whole note.
The head is hollow.
It does not have a stem.

This is a half note.
The head is hollow.
It has a stem.

This is a quarter note.
The head is solid.
It has a stem.

This is an eighth note,
The head is solid.
It has a stem and a flag.

This is a sixteenth note.
The head is solid.
It has a stem and two flags.

This is a thirty-second note.
The head is solid.
It has a stem and three flags.

RESTS:

A REST is a sign used to designate a period of silence.

This period of silence will be of the same duration of time as the note to which it corresponds.

This is a thirty-second rest.

This is a sixteenth rest

This is an eighth rest

This is a quarter rest

This is a half rest. Note that it lays on the line.

This is a whole rest. Note that it hangs down from the line.

NOTES:

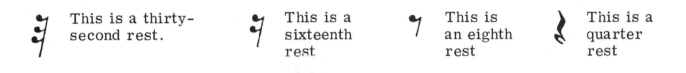

| WHOLE | HALF | QUARTER | EIGHTH | SIXTEENTH | THIRTY-SECOND |
|-------|------|---------|--------|-----------|---------------|

RESTS:

When the head of a note is placed above the third line, the stem is usually drawn downward on the left side of the note. When the head of the note is located below the third line the stem usually goes upward on the right side. Notes on the third line may have stems going either way. Practice writing different note and rest values.

Two or more notes with flags can be connected as shown:

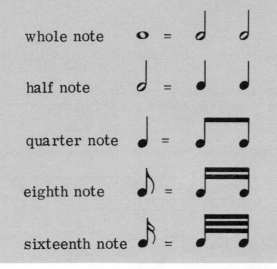

Practice writing eighth and sixteenth notes in the two ways shown. Pay very close attention to making your notation legible and easy to read.

The duration of the various notes is based upon a system of relative values. The chart below gives examples of this.

whole note ○ = 𝅗𝅥 𝅗𝅥

half note 𝅗𝅥 = ♩ ♩

quarter note ♩ = ♫

eighth note ♪ =

sixteenth note ♬ =

Triplets (a group of three notes performed in the time of two) may also be demonstrated with a chart showing relative values.

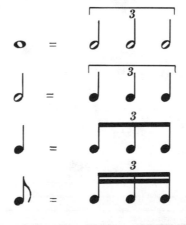

REMEMBER: A <u>Note</u> represents the <u>Pitch</u> and <u>Duration</u> of a tone and it will bear the name of the line or space it occupies on the staff.

A <u>Dot</u> <u>After</u> <u>A</u> <u>Note</u> (or a rest) increases its value by <u>one half</u>.
See the following examples.

Write three notes or rests which equal each of the following:

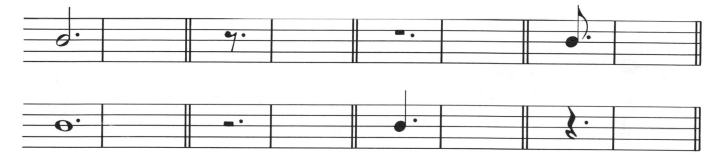

A Quick Review:

How many: (Questions 11-20)

1. _____ half notes = a 𝅝

2. _____ eighth notes = a 𝅗𝅥

3. _____ 𝄿 = a 𝄼

4. 4 quarter notes = _____ 𝅝

5. _____ quarter notes = 𝅗𝅥·

6. 2 eighth rests = _____ 𝄿

7. 𝅝· = _____ half notes

8. 𝅘𝅥𝅮· = _____ sixteenth notes

9. 𝅗𝅥 = _____ quarter notes

10. 𝄻 = _____ quarter rests

11. 𝅘𝅥𝅮 = 𝅝· _____

12. 𝅘𝅥𝅯 = 𝅘𝅥·  _____

13. 𝅘𝅥 = 𝅗𝅥  _____

14. 𝄼 = 𝅗𝅥  _____

15. 𝄿 = 𝄾·  _____

16. 𝅘𝅥𝅮· = 𝅝·  _____

17. 𝅘𝅥𝅯 = 𝅘𝅥𝅮·  _____

18. 𝅘𝅥𝅮 = 𝅘𝅥·  _____

19. 𝅘𝅥𝅯 = 𝅗𝅥  _____

20. 𝄿 = 𝄾  _____

The STAFF is divided into measures by vertical lines called BARS.

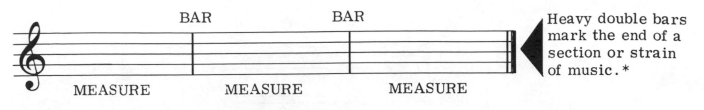

BAR    BAR

Heavy double bars mark the end of a section or strain of music.*

MEASURE  MEASURE  MEASURE

* A division within a piece or movement is shown by a light double bar.

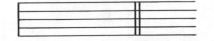

Note: A <u>measure</u> is the space between two bar lines.

The above examples are some common types of time signatures.

 The top number indicates the number of beats per measure.

 The bottom number indicates the type of note receiving one beat.

Example:

4 Beats per measure

4 A quarter-note receives one beat

 Signifies so called "common time" and is simply another way of designating $\frac{4}{4}$ time.

The symbol for cut time is ¢ . It means to give each note ½ of its written value. For our purposes all we need remember is that when the time signature ¢ appears, we will count $\frac{2}{2}$ instead of $\frac{4}{4}$ or ¢ .

On the following staff, write a number of Meter (Time signature) examples.

Simple Meter is when the upper number of the time signature is 2, 3, or 4.

Compound Meter is when the upper number of the time signature is 6, 9, or 12.

Meter, in general, is the regular recurrence of both accented and non-accented notes grouped into measures.

For example:

Duple Meter - 2 Beats    Beat 1 (Accent) Beat 2 (Non-accent)

Triple Meter - 3 Beats    Beat 1 (Accent) Beat 2 (Non-accent) Beat 3 (Non-accent)

Quadruple Meter - 4 Beats Beat 1 (Accent) Beat 2 (Non-accent) Beat 3 (Accent) Beat 4 (Non-accent)

Rhythm, in general, can be defined as the organized arrangement of sounds and silence. This includes anything connected with "motion" in music. (For example: Accent, Meter, and tempo.)

Tempo is the rate of movement or speed of a piece of music. Tempo is indicated by a word or phrase which is very often in Italian.
Some of the most important of these terms are given in the chart below. They are arranged in order from slowest to fastest.*

| | |
|---|---|
| Grave - Very, very slow | Moderato |
| Largo - Very slow | Allegretto |
| Larghetto | Allegro |
| Lento | Presto - Very fast |
| Adagio | Prestissimo - Very, very fast |
| Andante | |

* Tempo is measured with a metronome, a mechanical (or electric) device for determining the number of beats to be played at the tempo indicated by the composer. Set the metronome using the various tempo markings from the above list and listen so that a feeling for these may be established. Specific metronome markings may appear also as the following examples show.

m.m. ♩ = 70 Seventy metronome beats per minute; a quarter note receives one beat.
m.m. ♩ = 40 Forty metronome beats per minute; a half note receives one beat.

In the following examples, insert the correct time signature (meter).

In the following examples, insert Barlines to correctly divide each one into measures.

On a preceding page we learned that we could change $\frac{4}{4}$ (common) time to $\frac{2}{2}$ (cut) time. We can perform a similar change from "slow time" to "fast time" for $\frac{3}{8}$ - $\frac{6}{8}$ - $\frac{9}{8}$ - $\frac{12}{8}$ time by dividing both the top number of beats per measure and the value of the eighth note by 3, giving the eighth note ( ♪ ) $\frac{1}{3}$ beat.

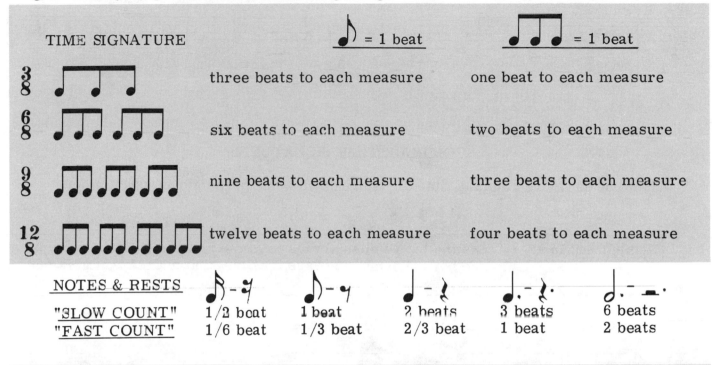

| TIME SIGNATURE | ♪ = 1 beat | ♪♪♪ = 1 beat |
|---|---|---|
| $\frac{3}{8}$ | three beats to each measure | one beat to each measure |
| $\frac{6}{8}$ | six beats to each measure | two beats to each measure |
| $\frac{9}{8}$ | nine beats to each measure | three beats to each measure |
| $\frac{12}{8}$ | twelve beats to each measure | four beats to each measure |

| NOTES & RESTS | | | | | |
|---|---|---|---|---|---|
| "SLOW COUNT" | 1/2 beat | 1 beat | 2 beats | 3 beats | 6 beats |
| "FAST COUNT" | 1/6 beat | 1/3 beat | 2/3 beat | 1 beat | 2 beats |

SYNCOPATION: Special rhythmic effects may be acquired in music by placing special accents ( > ) or emphasis on different beats or parts of a beat. If a natural accent or strong beat is moved from its normal place to a weak beat, we have syncopation. This could be done a number of ways. Study the following examples for some of them. (The accent marks are to show where syncopation occurs.)

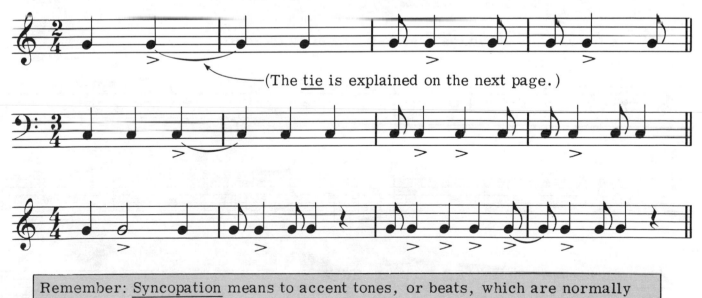

(The tie is explained on the next page.)

Remember: Syncopation means to accent tones, or beats, which are normally unaccented.

The <u>TIE</u> is a curved line between two notes of the same pitch.
The first note is played and held for the time duration of both.
The second note is not played but held.

Example:

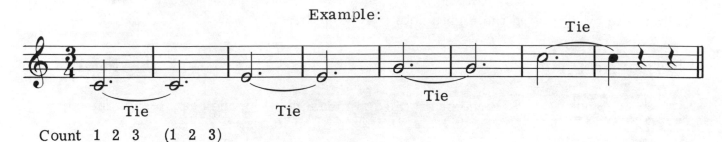

Count 1 2 3   (1 2 3)

## COMPLEX TIME SIGNATURES

Some of the more complex time signatures which are presently in use are:

$\frac{3}{2}$   $\frac{5}{4}$   $\frac{7}{4}$   $\frac{9}{4}$   $\frac{5}{8}$   $\frac{7}{8}$

> <u>Remember</u>: In every case the top number always tells the number of beats in a measure, and the bottom number always tens the kind of note that gets one beat.

Draw the missing bar lines in the following exercises.

Write the accents above the syncopated notes in these exercises.

18

# DURATION OF NOTES AND RESTS AND METER
## (REVIEW)

1. Determine the meter signatures and insert bar lines in the proper places.

2. Complete the time values in the following measures, using either notes or rests.

3. Complete the following measures so that they agree with the meter signature.

# KEY SIGNATURES--MAJOR
# AND MINOR SCALES

A <u>half step</u> is the distance from one pitch (tone) to the next nearest pitch (tone) either up or down. This interval is often referred to as a <u>semitone</u>.

Examples:

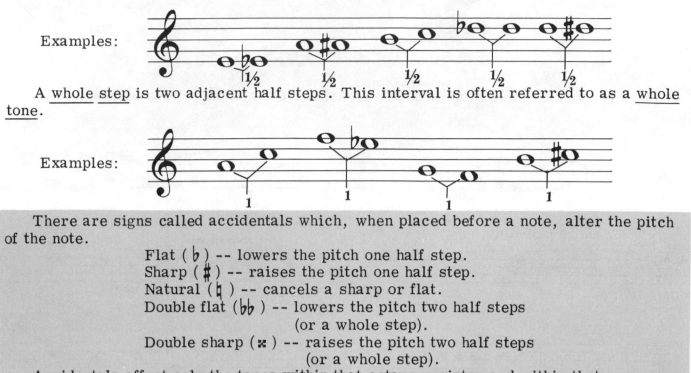

A <u>whole step</u> is two adjacent half steps. This interval is often referred to as a <u>whole tone</u>.

Examples:

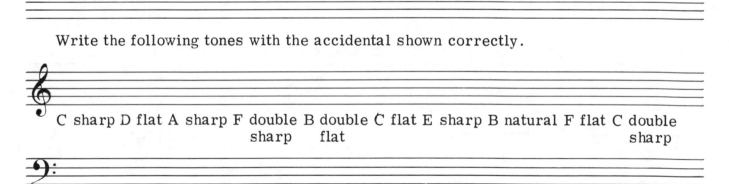

There are signs called accidentals which, when placed before a note, alter the pitch of the note.

Flat ( ♭ ) -- lowers the pitch one half step.
Sharp ( ♯ ) -- raises the pitch one half step.
Natural ( ♮ ) -- cancels a sharp or flat.
Double flat ( ♭♭ ) -- lowers the pitch two half steps
                  (or a whole step).
Double sharp ( 𝄪 ) -- raises the pitch two half steps
                  (or a whole step).

Accidentals affect only the tones within that octave register and within that measure.

Practice writing examples of the above shown accidentals.

Write the following tones with the accidental shown correctly.

C sharp  D flat  A sharp  F double  B double  C flat  E sharp  B natural  F flat  C double
                      sharp    flat                                        sharp

B sharp  E double  G sharp  B flat  A flat  A natural  E flat  D sharp  C natural  G flat  D natural
          flat

Sharps and flats immediately following the clef sign are called the <u>key signature</u>. These accidentals affect every note on the line or space which they represent throughout the entire composition unless they are cancelled by a natural sign (♮) or a change to another key.

In the following example, every note called F is now raised one half-step to F♯ because a sharp is placed on the F line in the key signature.

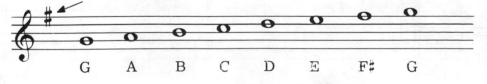

G    A    B    C    D    E    F♯    G

In the following example all notes called B - E - A are now lowered one half-step to B♭ -E♭ -A♭ because flats have been placed on the B line, E space, and A space in the key signature.

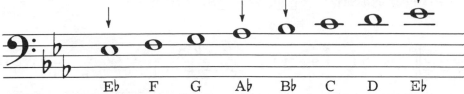

Eb    F    G    Ab    Bb    C    D    Eb

A <u>Diatonic Scale</u> is a series of eight successive notes (the eighth duplicating the first) that are arranged in a systematic relationship of whole and half steps.

The diatonic scale is made up of two types -- <u>Major</u> and <u>Minor</u>.

In the Major scale the half steps occur between the 3-4 and 7-8 tones of the scale. All of the rest of the tones progress by whole steps.

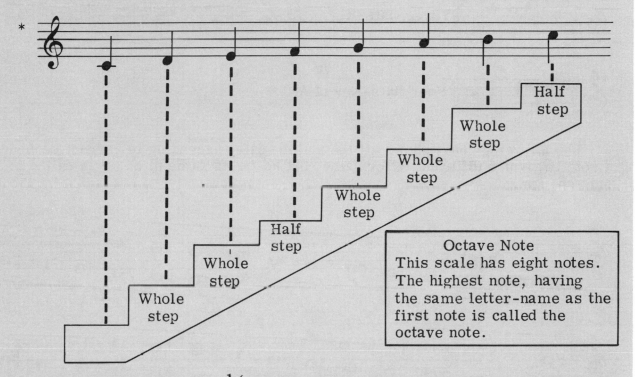

Octave Note
This scale has eight notes. The highest note, having the same letter-name as the first note is called the octave note.

* When a scale is written with the ½ steps from the 3rd to 4th and 7th to 8th steps of the scale, it is a major scale, and is given the name of the <u>first note</u>.

In order to produce the major scales in "Sharp" keys, select a new starting tone five steps above the last starting tone and raise each new seventh scale step by means of a sharp.

Study the resulting major sharp <u>Key Signatures</u>.

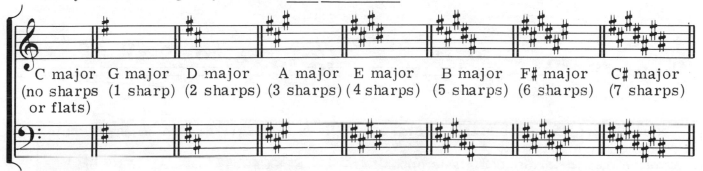

C major   G major   D major    A major   E major    B major    F♯ major    C♯ major
(no sharps (1 sharp) (2 sharps) (3 sharps) (4 sharps) (5 sharps) (6 sharps) (7 sharps)
 or flats)

In order to produce the major scales in the "flat" keys, select a new starting tone five scale steps <u>down</u> from the last starting tone and flat the new fourth scale tone. (Keep all flats from the previous key signature.)

Study the resulting major flat <u>key</u> signatures.

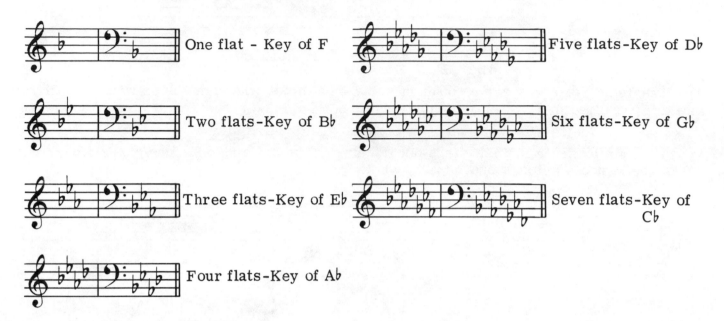

One flat - Key of F

Two flats-Key of B♭

Three flats-Key of E♭

Four flats-Key of A♭

Five flats-Key of D♭

Six flats-Key of G♭

Seven flats-Key of C♭

The following chart shows <u>all</u> the major scales ascending in correct sequence. (When a note is given a different letter name, but keeps its same pitch, it is called an <u>enharmonic</u> change.)

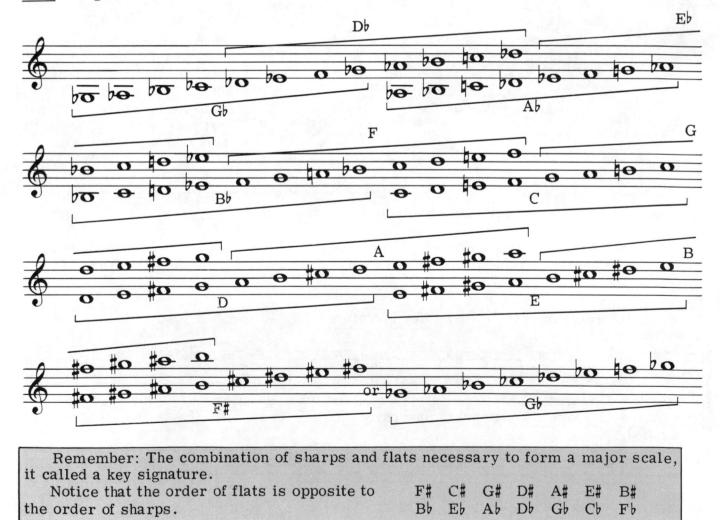

Remember: The combination of sharps and flats necessary to form a major scale, it called a key signature.

Notice that the order of flats is opposite to the order of sharps.

| F♯ | C♯ | G♯ | D♯ | A♯ | E♯ | B♯ |
|----|----|----|----|----|----|----|
| B♭ | E♭ | A♭ | D♭ | G♭ | C♭ | F♭ |

# A TABLE OF MAJOR KEYS AND SIGNATURES

C MAJOR has no sharps or flats

| | | | | | | | |
|---|---|---|---|---|---|---|---|
| G MAJOR has one sharp, | F♯ | | | | | | |
| D MAJOR has two sharps, | F♯ | C♯ | | | | | |
| A MAJOR has three sharps, | F♯ | C♯ | G♯ | | | | |
| E MAJOR has four sharps, | F♯ | C♯ | G♯ | D♯ | | | |
| B MAJOR has five sharps, | F♯ | C♯ | G♯ | D♯ | A♯ | | |
| F♯ MAJOR has six sharps, | F♯ | C♯ | G♯ | D♯ | A♯ | E♯ | |
| C♯ MAJOR has seven sharps, | F♯ | C♯ | G♯ | D♯ | A♯ | E♯ | B♯ |

| | | | | | | | |
|---|---|---|---|---|---|---|---|
| F MAJOR has one flat, | B♭ | | | | | | |
| B♭ MAJOR has two flats, | B♭ | E♭ | | | | | |
| E♭ MAJOR has three flats, | B♭ | E♭ | A♭ | | | | |
| A♭ MAJOR has four flats, | B♭ | E♭ | A♭ | D♭ | | | |
| D♭ MAJOR has five flats, | B♭ | E♭ | A♭ | D♭ | G♭ | | |
| G♭ MAJOR has six flats, | B♭ | E♭ | A♭ | D♭ | G♭ | C♭ | |
| C♭ MAJOR has seven flats, | B♭ | E♭ | A♭ | D♭ | G♭ | C♭ | F♭ |

The following diagram of the cycle of keys
shows the relationship of all the major scales.

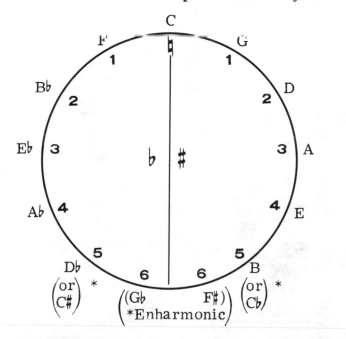

The most important degrees
in each key are 1-3-5 which
form the Tonic or I chord of
the key.

Write the 1-3-5 or <u>Tonic</u> of
the following keys:
C, G, F, A, E♭ , and B.

STARTING WITH C, MOVING TO THE
RIGHT GIVES US THE KEYS CONTAINING
SHARPS AND MOVING TO THE LEFT
GIVES US THE KEYS CONTAINING FLATS.

*Enharmonic: Written differently as to
notation but sounding the same.

# CONSTRUCTING MAJOR SCALES

Construct the Major Scale for each key and LABEL THE ROOT, 3RD, and 5TH Tones of each scale. Finally, write the Sharps or Flats found in each Key.

# MINOR SCALES

Each Major key will have a Relative Minor key.
The Relative Minor Scale is built upon the sixth tone of the Major Scale.
The Key Signature of both will be the same.
The Minor Scale will have the same number of tones (7) as the Major.
The difference between the scales is the arrangement of the whole-steps and half-steps.
There are three forms of the minor scale: 1. PURE or NATURAL, 2. HARMONIC, 3. MELODIC.

## THE MAJOR AND RELATIVE MINOR KEYS

| | | C | Am | | |
|---|---|---|---|---|---|
| D is the 6th Tone of the F Scale; G is the 6th Tone of the B Scale, etc. | F | Dm | | F♯ | D♯m |
| | B♭ | Gm | | B | G♯m |
| | E♭ | Cm | | E | C♯m |
| | A♭ | Fm | | A | F♯m |
| | D♭ | B♭m | | D | Bm |
| | G♭ | E♭m | | G | Em |

The NATURAL or PURE MINOR SCALE begins on the 6th degree of its relative major scale and ascends or descends for one octave using the key signature of the major scale. We usually use small letters to indicate minor keys. The half steps occur between 2-3 and 5-6.

c minor (natural)

The HARMONIC MINOR SCALE begins on the 6th degree of its relative major scale and ascends or descends for one octave using the key signature of the major scale except that the 7th tone is raised 1/2 step. (See arrow in the example below) The half steps occur between 2-3, 5-6, and 7-8.*

c minor (harmonic)

* The raised seventh scale tone in the harmonic minor creates the distance of a step and one half between 6-7.

The MELODIC MINOR SCALE also begins on the 6th degree of its relative major scale and ascends or descends for one octave using the key signature of the major scale except that in ascending the 6th and 7th tones are raised 1/2 step and in descending the 6th and 7th tones return to the natural or pure minor scale form.*

c minor (melodic)

* In the melodic minor ascending, the half steps occur between the 2-3 and 7-8 scale tones. When descending, between 6-5 and 3-2. The descending melodic form is actually the form of a <u>pure</u> minor scale.

# CONSTRUCTING MINOR SCALES

Construct the following Minor Scales and show the ROOT, THIRD, and 5th of each scale. Pay close attention to the Minor Third in each scale. Show both ascending and descending forms of the melodic minor.*

a pure minor (relative major = <u>C</u> )   a harmonic minor

a melodic minor

b pure minor (relative major = ___ )   b harmonic minor

b melodic minor

f pure minor (relative major = ___ )   f harmonic minor

f melodic minor

c# pure minor (relative major = ___ )   c# harmonic minor

c# melodic minor

eb pure minor (relative major = ___ )   eb harmonic minor

eb melodic minor

g# pure minor (relative major = ___ )   g# harmonic minor

g# melodic minor

* The student should continue to write the minor scales in the remaining keys on staff paper. Remember that frequent drill in any phase of music fundamentals is necessary!

Summary of minor scales:

1. Relative minor scales are constructed upon the sixth scale tone of the related major scales and have the same key signatures.

2. The first five tones of the three forms of the minor scales are the same in any given key.

3. The seventh scale tone of the pure minor is raised to form the harmonic minor scale. This accidental is not included in the key signature.

4. The sixth and seventh scale tones of the pure minor are raised in ascending and lowered in descending to form the melodic minor scale. The accidentals used in the ascending form to raise 6-7 are not included in the key signature.

A CHROMATIC SCALE is a scale which consists entirely of half steps. It may be written by the use of accidentals (♯ - ♭ - ♮ ) in connection with the regular key signature. Sharp and natural signs are used for the ascending scale and flat and natural signs for the descending scale.

The filled-in notes designate the ascending and descending chromatic tones in C major in the following example:

Write an ascending chromatic scale in the key of E♭ on the following staff.

Write a descending chromatic scale in the key of A on the following staff.

Notice that the chromatic scale has a number of <u>enharmonic</u> tones (see page 23). The term enharmonic pertains to tones which are "Spelled" differently but sound the same. For example: a♭ - g♯ ; c♭ - b; e♭ - d♯ ; and f♭ - e.

Write enharmonic equivalents of the tones given below:
Example:

# KEY SIGNATURES--MAJOR
# AND MINOR SCALES
## (REVIEW)

1. Put in the clef sign, write the proper key signature and place the starting note of the scale in the following exercises.

Treble Clef

A          G♭          B          E♭

Bass Clef

D          B♭          A          G♭

2. Write the name of the key below the following examples and place the starting note of the scale on the staff.

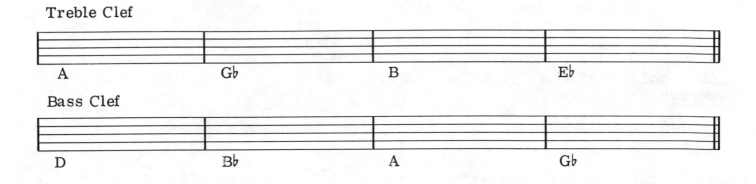

3. Using half notes write the MAJOR SCALES ascending and descending for the following key signatures.

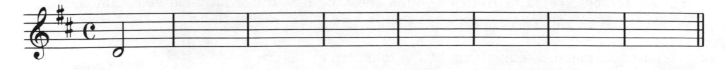

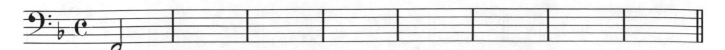

28

4. Determine the relative minor keys of the following Major Keys. (use small letters and proper accidentals.)

| Major Scale | Relative minor Scale | Major Scale | Relative minor Scale |
|---|---|---|---|
| C | a | G | _____ |
| F | _____ | D | _____ |
| Bb | _____ | A | _____ |
| Eb | _____ | E | _____ |
| Ab | _____ | B | _____ |
| Db | _____ | F# | _____ |
| Gb | _____ | C# | _____ |
| Cb | _____ | | |

5. Name the following Major Scales; then name and write the relative minor scale of each, as indicated, both ascending and descending.

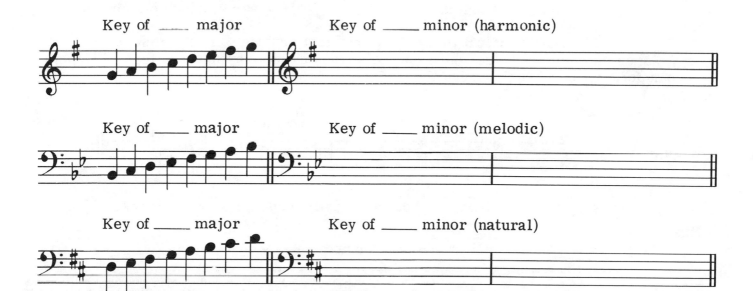

Key of _____ major    Key of _____ minor (harmonic)

Key of _____ major    Key of _____ minor (melodic)

Key of _____ major    Key of _____ minor (natural)

6. On the staff below, write the enharmonic note in the second measure.

7. How many notes are there in a chromatic scale including the octave?_____

8. What is the interval between the tones of the chromatic scale?_____

9. Write the chromatic half steps above and below the following tones.

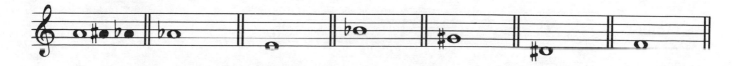

# FORM AND EXPRESSION MARKS

In order to read, write, or understand music, one must know all of the signs, words and abbreviations which are often referred to as the musical vocabulary. Many of these have been given in other chapters, but most are included here.

1. A melody is a succession of single tones.

2. A chord is a combination of tones sounded together.

3. A triad is a three note chord.

Tones in a melody.          The same tones as a chord.

4. A phrase is a short musical thought -- a musical sentence. The phrase usually finishes on a note of longer duration, or at the end of a rhythmic pattern. A double bar does not necessarily mean the beginning or end of a phrase.

Example:

5. A period is a "complete musical thought" usually made up of two phrases.

Example:

6. A slur is a curved line drawn above or below groups of two or more notes. Usually this means that the notes are to be played or sung legato (Smoothly).

Example:

7. A tie is a curved line connecting two notes of the same letter name and pitch.

Example:

8. When sections or portions of a piece of music are to be repeated, various signs are used.

(A) <u>D.C.</u> (Da Capo) means to repeat from the beginning to the word <u>Fine</u> (the end).

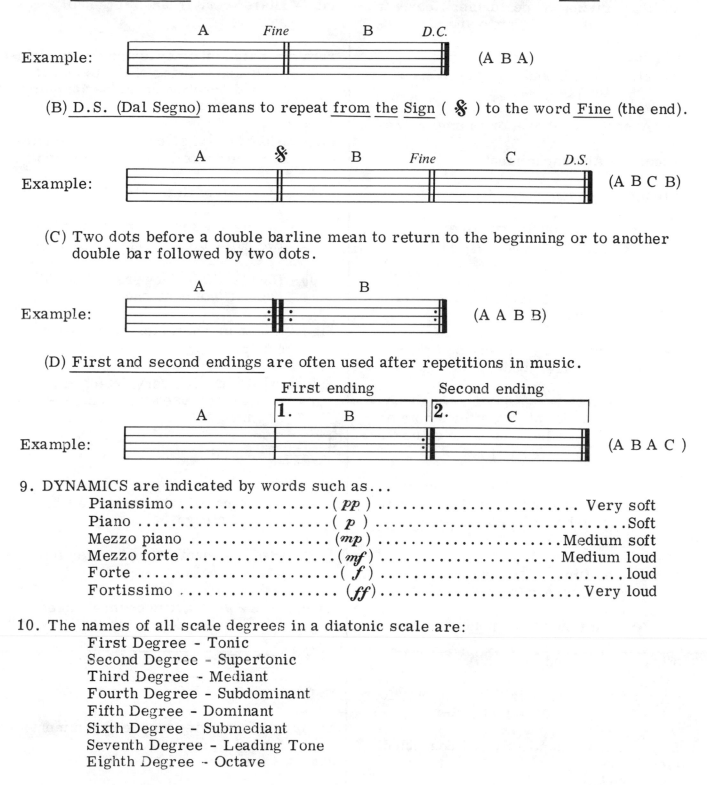

Example:                              (A B A)

(B) <u>D.S.</u> (Dal Segno) means to repeat <u>from the Sign</u> ( 𝄋 ) to the word <u>Fine</u> (the end).

Example:                              (A B C B)

(C) Two dots before a double barline mean to return to the beginning or to another double bar followed by two dots.

Example:                              (A A B B)

(D) <u>First and second endings</u> are often used after repetitions in music.

Example:                              (A B A C )

9. DYNAMICS are indicated by words such as...
    Pianissimo .................... ( *pp* ) ......................... Very soft
    Piano ........................ ( *p* ) ............................ Soft
    Mezzo piano ................. ( *mp* ) ....................... Medium soft
    Mezzo forte ................. ( *mf* ) ...................... Medium loud
    Forte ........................ ( *f* ) ............................ loud
    Fortissimo ................. ( *ff* ) ...................... Very loud

10. The names of all scale degrees in a diatonic scale are:
    First Degree - Tonic
    Second Degree - Supertonic
    Third Degree - Mediant
    Fourth Degree - Subdominant
    Fifth Degree - Dominant
    Sixth Degree - Submediant
    Seventh Degree - Leading Tone
    Eighth Degree - Octave

# ADDITIONAL EXPRESSION MARKS AND DEFINITIONS

ad lib. - giving the performer liberty in matters of tempo and expression.

Accel. - Accelerando (increase speed or tempo)

ᵖ Accent - to stress or to emphasize

Accom. - Accompaniment

a tempo - resume strict time

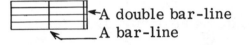 ←A double bar-line
← A bar-line

V , ' - Breath marks

⊕ - Coda

◁ or cresc. - crescendo (get louder)

• - Dot
1) a dot placed after a note or rest increases the value one half. (Exp. ♩. )

2) a dot placed below or above a note indicates that the note should be played staccato. (Exp. ♩ )

▷ or Dim. - Diminuendo or Decresc. (get softer)

⌢ - a fermata or hold

Fine - the end

♩ (Subdivide) - in this case play four eighth notes.

Leg. - Legato (smoothly and connected)
meno - less
ped. - pedal
piu - more
rall. - rallentando (gradually slower)
repeat - a character indicating that certain measures or passages are to be sung or played twice. (see previous page)

rit. - ritard or ritardando (gradually slower)

rubato - a flexibility of tempo - a quickening and slowing of the tempo at the discretion of the performer or conductor.

sforzando (sfz) - a strong accent - immediately followed by piano (soft).

♯ ; ♭ ; ♮ - sharp; flat; natural

✕ - Double - Sharp ; raises the pitch two half-steps or one whole step.

♭♭ - Double - flat ; lowers the pitch two half steps or one whole step.

Sign - a note or character employed in music.

Spiccato - Italian for very detached. (usually used for string instruments.)

≣ - a staff

Suspension - the holding of a note in any chord into the chord which follows

♩ or ten. - tenuto - sustain for full value.

Triplet - ♩♩♩ - a group of three notes performed in the time of 2.

Tutti - All - Everyone sings or plays.

Unis. - Unison

Vamp - to improvise an accompaniment

8va. - 8 notes higher

Voce (It.) - the voice

Volume - The power (loudness or softness) of a voice or instrument

Whole step - two half steps or a major second

# FORM AND
# EXPRESSION MARKS
## (REVIEW)

1. A three note chord is called a _____ .

2. A succession of single tones is called a _____ .

3. A phrase is _____ .

4. A period is _____ .

5. Match the following by putting the correct letter in the blank.

_____ Mezzo forte      A. very loud
_____ Piano      B. very soft
_____ Mezzo piano      C. med. loud
_____ Forte      D. med. soft
_____ Pianissimo      E. soft
_____ Fortissimo      F. loud

6. Fill in the correct names of the scale degrees in a diatonic scale.

First Degree _____      Fifth Degree _____
Second Degree _____      Sixth Degree _____
Third Degree _____      Seventh Degree _____
Fourth Degree _____      Eighth Degree _____

7. Match the following terms with the correct definitions.

_____ slur
_____ chord
_____ Dal Segno (D.S.)
_____ tie
_____ a tempo
_____ rall.
_____ Tutti
_____ 8va.
_____ volume
_____ ad. lib.
_____ accent
_____ crescendo
_____ sforzando ( $sfz$ )
_____ decrescendo
_____ Da Capo (D.C.)

A. repeat from the beginning to the word Fine
B. 8 notes higher
C. curved line drawn above or below groups of two or more notes.
D. strong accent immediately followed by piano ( $p$ )
E. gradually slower
F. combination of tones sounded together
G. get softer
H. All-everyone sings or plays
I. curved line connecting two notes of the same letter name and pitch
J. giving the performer liberty of tempo and expression
K. resume strict time
L. repeat from the sign ( $\S$ ) to the word Fine
M. loudness or softness of a voice or instrument
N. to stress or emphasize
O. get louder

# INTERVALS AND TWO-PART HARMONY

An <u>interval</u> in music is the distance between two tones with regard to pitch. The interval is counted from the lower note to the upper, including both notes. Intervals remain the same whether we use the bass clef or the treble clef.

Intervals played or written together are called Harmonic.

Intervals played or written one after another are called Melodic.

INTERVALS IN THE SCALE OF C MAJOR

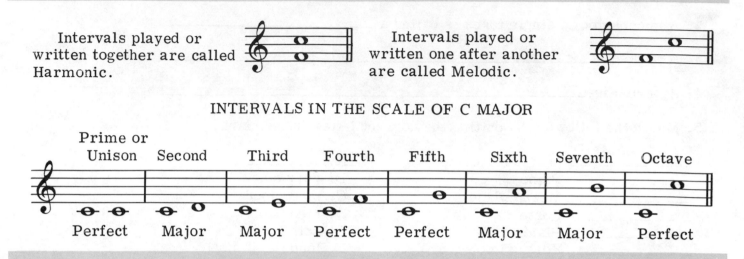

An Interval is Major when the upper note is found in the major scale of the lower note.

Example: is major because G♯ belongs to the major scale of E.

Write the interval name under the notes in the following exercise.

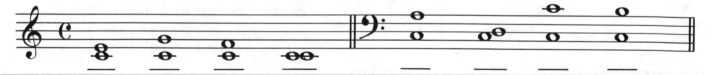

When the distance between two notes of a Major interval is made one half step smaller, it is called a MINOR INTERVAL.

Only SECONDS - THIRDS - SIXTHS - SEVENTHS or Major intervals can be made minor.
Examples:

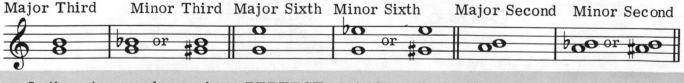

In the minor scales we have PERFECT, MAJOR and MINOR INTERVALS.

Which of the following intervals are major and which are minor?

The following are examples of a harmonic minor scale and a melodic minor scale showing all intervals in the key of D minor.

Harmonic d minor Scale.

Per. Prime   Maj. 2nd   m 3rd   Per. 4th   Per. 5th   m 6th   Maj. 7th   Per. 8th

Melodic d minor Scale - Ascending.

Per. Prime   Maj. 2nd   m 3rd   Per. 4th   Per. 5th   Maj. 6th   Maj. 7th   Per. 8th

Melodic d minor Scale - Descending.

Per. 8th   m 7th   m 6th   Per. 5th   Per. 4th   m 3rd   Maj. 2nd   Per. Prime

Identify the following general intervals:

Write the indicated intervals above the following tones: (Assume at present that each given note is the starting note, or tonic, of a scale.)

M2   M2   P4   P5   M6   M7   P8   P4

P8   M3   P4   M7   P5   M6   M2   P8

Change the following major intervals to minor.

If a perfect or a major interval is expanded by a half step it becomes <u>augmented</u>.

Examples:

P4  A4   P5  A5   M2  A2   M6  A6

If a perfect interval is contracted by a half step, it then becomes <u>diminished</u>; While if a major interval is contracted a half step, it becomes <u>minor</u>.

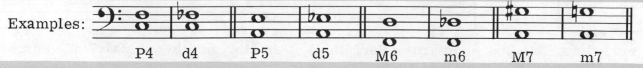

Examples:

P4  d4   P5  d5   M6  m6   M7  m7

If a <u>major</u> interval is made <u>minor</u> and then contracted another half step, it becomes <u>diminished</u>.

Example:

M3  m3  d3

The four most common <u>Augmented Intervals</u> are as follows:

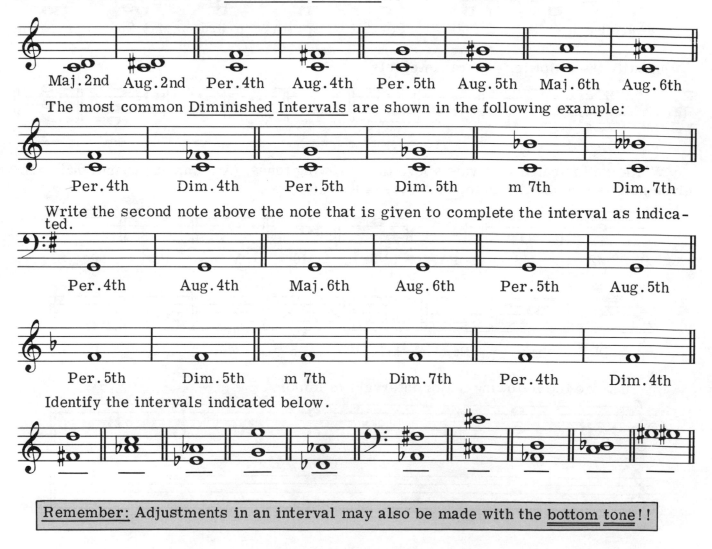

Maj.2nd  Aug.2nd  Per.4th  Aug.4th  Per.5th  Aug.5th  Maj.6th  Aug.6th

The most common <u>Diminished Intervals</u> are shown in the following example:

Per.4th  Dim.4th  Per.5th  Dim.5th  m 7th  Dim.7th

Write the second note above the note that is given to complete the interval as indicated.

Per.4th  Aug.4th  Maj.6th  Aug.6th  Per.5th  Aug.5th

Per.5th  Dim.5th  m 7th  Dim.7th  Per.4th  Dim.4th

Identify the intervals indicated below.

Remember: Adjustments in an interval may also be made with the <u>bottom tone</u>!!

The <u>inversion</u> of an interval is the result of moving one of the tones an octave while the other tone remains stationary. When an interval is inverted its character is changed.

When intervals are inverted:

1. These changes take place in the interval name.

   prime (or unison) becomes octave      fifth becomes fourth
   second becomes seventh      sixth becomes third
   third becomes sixth      seventh becomes second
   fourth becomes fifth      octave becomes prime (or unison)

2. The qualities change as follows:

   major becomes minor      diminished becomes augmented
   minor becomes major      augmented becomes diminished

3. All qualities are reversed except <u>perfect</u>.

Examples:

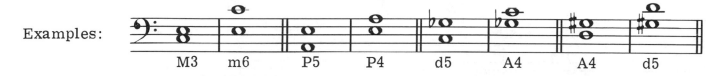

Write the inversion of each of the following intervals and name it.

Intervals are examples of the simplest harmony used in music. This is often called <u>two-part</u> <u>harmony</u>. In its most uncomplicated state a melody would be harmonized with a second part written a "third" or a "sixth" lower than the melody.

Examples: (The second part is written a "third" lower.)

(The second part is written a "sixth" lower.)

Harmonize the following melody with a second part a "third" lower.

# INTERVALS AND TWO-PART HARMONY
## (REVIEW)

1. Write five examples of each of the following intervals. MINOR THIRD: MAJOR SECOND: MINOR SIXTH: MAJOR SEVENTH.

Minor third        Major second

Minor sixth        Major seventh

2. Name each of the following intervals.

3. Identify all the intervals and write their inversions.

M3   m6

4. Name the following intervals.

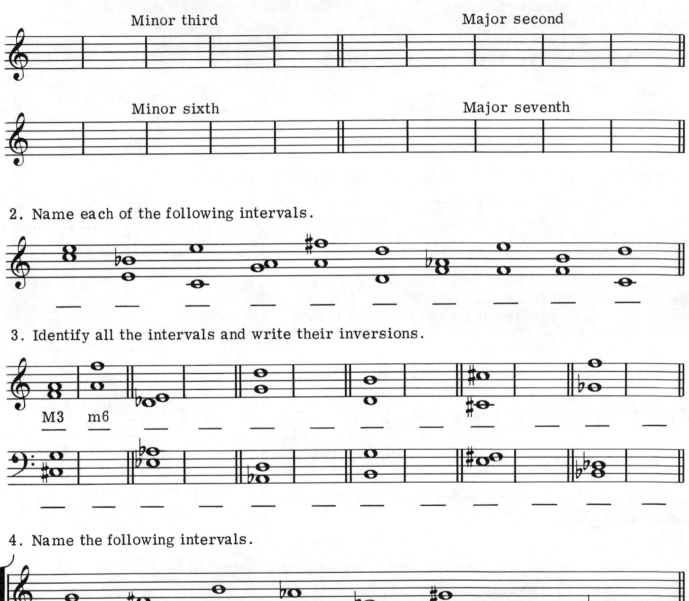

5. The most common AUGMENTED INTERVALS are: _____ _____ _____

6. The PERFECT INTERVALS in any Major scale are: _____

7. The MAJOR INTERVALS in any Major scale are: _____

8. The PERFECT INTERVALS in any minor scale are: _____

9. The MINOR INTERVALS in the harmonic form of any minor scale are: _____

10. The MAJOR INTERVALS in the harmonic form of any minor scale are: _____

11. Harmonize the following melody with the second part a "sixth" lower in the first four measures and a "third" lower in the last four measures.

12. Write the second note above the note that is given to complete the correct interval in the following exercises.

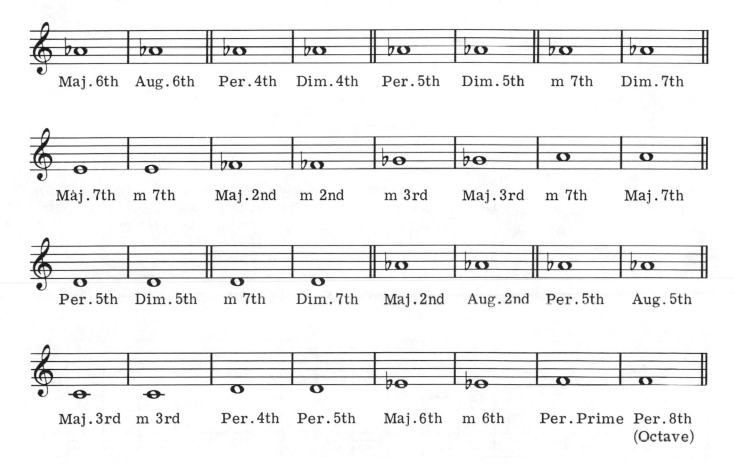

# TRANSPOSITION

Transposition is the act of changing music from one key to another key. The most widely used method of transposition is by interval. Very often, the purpose of transposition is to enable a performer to use one system of fingering for a whole family of differently pitched instruments. (In band or orchestral music, for example.) The interval of transposition is measured on the Grand Staff. (See preceding chapter for a discussion of intervals.)

In the following example we will transpose a short phrase from the Key of E♭ Major to the Key of G Major. Because the key of G Major is a third higher than the Key of E♭ Major, we will write each note of the melody a third higher.

Transpose the following melody from the Key of G Major to the keys indicated on the following staves.

All orchestral or band music today is written on one of four clefs. The treble (G) and Bass (F) clefs, of course, and also on one of two C clefs; the Alto and Tenor. The Alto clef (often called the Viola clef), is made by combining the two lower lines of the G clef, "middle C", and the two upper lines of the F clef. This portion of the Grand Staff is thus isolated on a staff of its own.

Rewrite the pitches from the G clef onto the Alto clef and then name them.

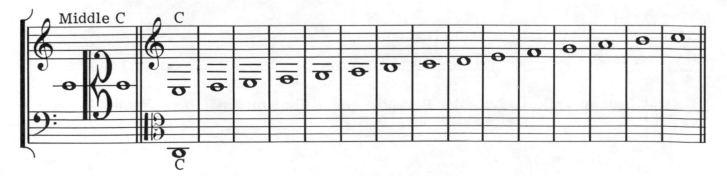

The Tenor Clef is constructed by taking the lowest line of the G clef, "Middle C", and the three upper lines of the F clef. This portion of the Grand Staff is isolated on a staff of its own.

Rewrite the pitches from the F clef onto the Tenor Clef and then name them.

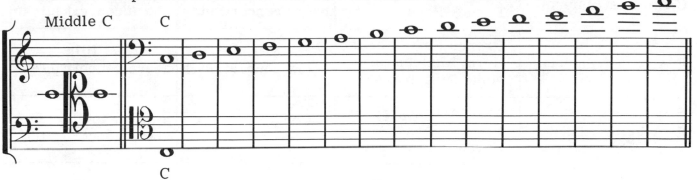

The Tenor Clef is often used by the cello, string bass, trombone, bassoon, and baritone horn.

Rewrite the following exercise into both the Alto and Tenor clefs.

A transposing instrument is one which sounds a pitch other than the one it reads. Another way to say it would be - it reads pitches other than it sounds. Instruments are very often labelled by the pitch of the scale they sound when they read a "C" scale. A B♭ instrument is one which sounds a B♭ scale when it reads a "C" scale. An E♭ is an instrument which sounds an E♭ scale when it reads a "C" scale. The interval of transposition is measured from "Middle C". Therefore, in order to be able to play "in tune" with the concert pitch, the composer or arranger must <u>transpose</u> some instruments <u>the same interval</u> above or below the concert pitch that the instrument sounds above or below that pitch. See the chart on pages 64 and 65.

The B♭ Soprano instruments include Clarinets, Cornets, Trumpets, and Saxophones. They sound a major second below "Middle C", so they must be written a major second above Middle C".

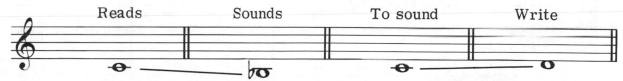

The A soprano instruments include clarinets, cornets, trumpets, and sometimes, French Horns. They sound a minor third below "Middle C", so they must be written a minor third above "Middle C".

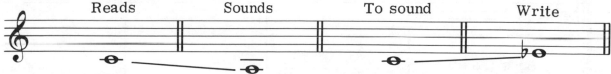

41

Some additional transposing instruments are as follows:

| Instruments | Group Includes: | They sound: | They must be written: |
|---|---|---|---|
| G Alto Instruments | Alto Flute; sometimes French Horn | perfect fourth below concert pitch | a perfect fourth above concert pitch |
| F Alto Instruments | French Horn; English Horn; Mellophone; some Saxophones | perfect fifth below concert pitch | a perfect fifth above concert pitch |
| E♭ Alto Instruments | Alto Saxophones; French Horns; Alto Horns; Mellophones | major sixth below concert pitch | a major sixth above concert pitch |
| C Tenor Instruments | Bass Flute; Baritone Oboe | octave below written pitch | no transposition necessary |

There are a number of other transposing instruments which are not nearly as common as those which have already been discussed, but if one is to write or arrange music for band or orchestra, then he must become familiar with the process. Once the "Key" of the instrument is known, then the composer or arranger may proceed in the manner outlined above. Ranges for various instruments are given in a chart on pages 64 and 65. (Remember this rule about transposition of brass instruments -- All brass instruments (except the French Horn), when written in the bass clef, are non-transposing instruments. All brass instruments, when written in the treble clef, are always transposing instruments.)

Transpose and/or arrange the following four measures for each of the following groups of instruments. Remember to add correct key signatures when transposing.

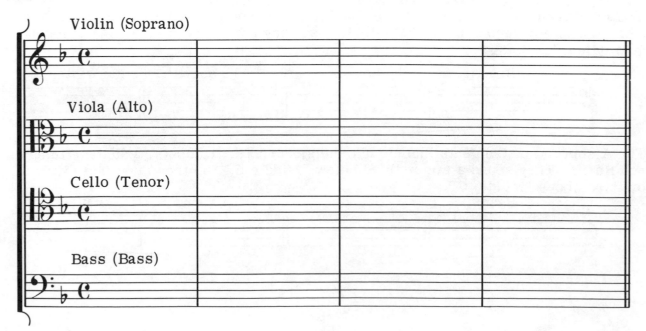

Bb Cornet (Soprano)

Eb Mellopone (Alto)

French Horn in F (Tenor)

Trombone (Bass)

C Flute (Soprano)

Bb Clarinet (Alto)

F English Horn (Tenor)

Bassoon (Bass)

Rewrite the following melody from alto into tenor clef.

Rewrite the following melody from tenor into bass clef.

# TRANSPOSITION
## (REVIEW)

1. Transpose the following melody from the key of G to the keys indicated.

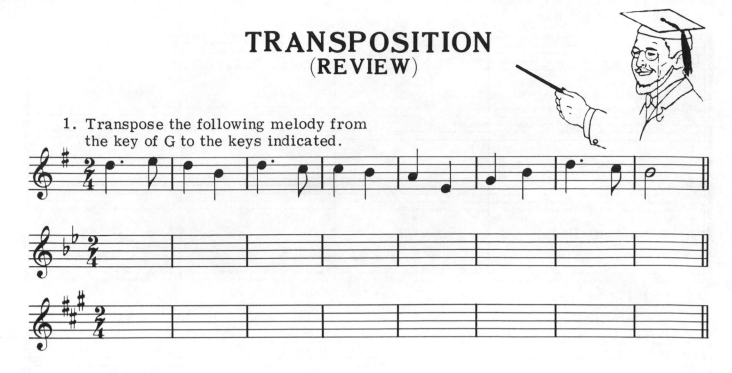

2. Rewrite the following melody into the alto clef.

3. Transpose the following melody from the Key of E♭ to the keys indicated.

4. Transpose this melody for G alto instruments to sound in unison with concert pitch.

Concert pitch

G Alto instruments

# TRIADS--TONIC AND DOMINANT

A <u>chord</u> consists of two or more tones sounded together. A <u>triad</u> is a chord using three tones.

There are four types of triads: major, minor, augmented, and diminished.

A major chord or triad contains a root, a major third, and a perfect fifth.

The following are major triads:

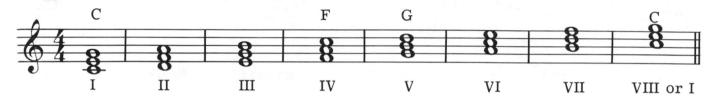

If we build a chord consisting of a root-third-fifth on every degree of a major scale, we will find three major chords.

In the following example, notice the use of ROMAN NUMERALS to help identify the scale degree.

The three major chords occur on the first, I, fourth, IV, and fifth, V, degrees of the major scale.

Construct major triads on the following tones:

Each scale degree has a name as well as a number. The first degree, which gives the tone of the key, is called the <u>Tonic</u>. The fifth degree is the "dominating" note of the scale, and is called the <u>Dominant</u>. The fourth degree is called the <u>Subdominant</u>. These three degrees are often referred to by name.

The names of all the scale degrees are as follows:

> First Degree - Tonic
> Second Degree - Supertonic
> Third Degree - Mediant
> Fourth Degree - Subdominant
> Fifth Degree - Dominant
> Sixth Degree - Submediant
> Seventh Degree - Leading Tone
> Eighth Degree - Octave

Write the Tonic and Dominant Triads in the major scales of G; F; C; B♭; and A. (Use accidentals before the notes that need them.)

The three triads (Tonic, Subdominant, and Dominant) discussed on the previous page are often called the <u>primary</u> or <u>principal</u> triads.

Write the primary triads in the major keys shown below:

Write the primary triads in the minor keys given below: (use the harmonic minor scale as a basis -- remember the raised seventh scale tone!)

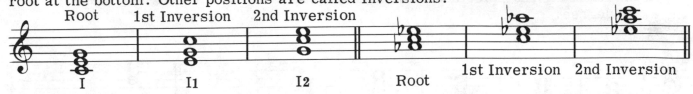

(For a more complete discussion of the <u>Subdominant</u> <u>chord</u> <u>see</u> <u>the</u> <u>next</u> <u>chapter.</u>)

Chords may be written in different positions. The original position always has the root at the bottom. Other positions are called Inversions.

Write the three positions of the Tonic Triads in the keys of G, F, D, B♭, E♭, E. Do not use signatures.

Simple choral harmony is usually written in four voices or parts. One way to do this would be to write the root of each chord in the bass. Since there are only three notes in a Tonic or a Dominant chord, one tone (usually the root) must be doubled. The movement of one chord to another is called a progression. In many <u>progressions</u> there is a common tone. It is usually best to keep the common tone in the same voice.

Examples:

Complete the following progressions.

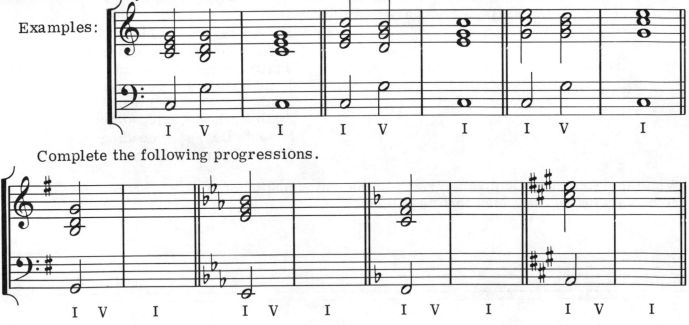

46

A cadence is the close or end of a phrase. The chord ending V to I, is called Authentic. When the root of the Tonic chord is in the top voice, it is called Perfect. If the third or fifth of the Tonic chord is in the top voice, it is called Imperfect.

Perfect authentic cadences

V       I

Imperfect authentic cadences

V      I      V      I

# TRIADS--TONIC AND DOMINANT
## (REVIEW)

1. Build a major chord on the first, fourth, and fifth degrees of the following keys. Mark the Roman Numeral below and the letter name above each chord.

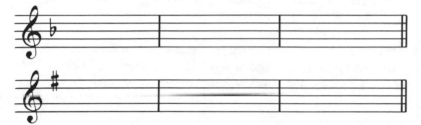

2. Fill in the missing note in the following major chords. Since there is no key signature indicated, it will be necessary to write in the proper accidentals (sharps or flats).

  Db      A      Ab      E      F#      Bb

3. Harmonize the following melodies.

I V I   I I I   V V I          I I   V I   V V   I

I I   V V   I V   I

# TRIADS-- (MINOR AND SUBDOMINANT)

A minor triad is comprised of a minor third and a perfect fifth.

Examples: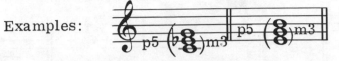

Construct minor triads on the following notes:

Minor Triads occur on the second, II, third, III, and sixth, VI, degrees of the major scale.

The following are various inversions of the minor triads in the key of C Major.

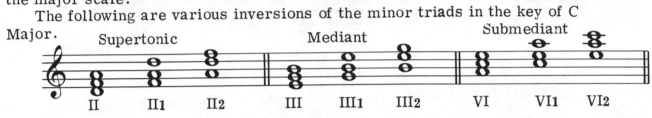

Remember -- a chord is inverted when any note other than the root is in the bass. When the fifth of any triad is in the bass, it is called a six-four chord. It takes its name from the intervals of which it is composed. Inversions of the minor triads are figured the same as major triads. In the 1st inversion, unlike major triads, the third may be doubled.

Examples: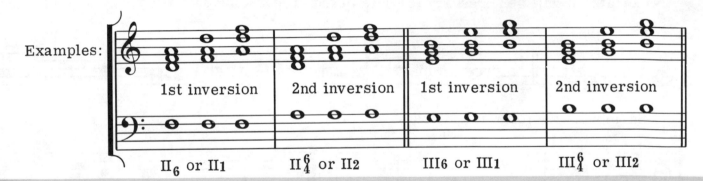

Chordal Progressions: The Supertonic, II, may follow the Tonic, I, or the Subdominant, IV. The Submediant, VI, may follow the Tonic, I, or the Dominant Seventh, $V_7$. The mediant, III, may follow the Tonic, I; or the Dominant, V.

Harmonize the following melody.

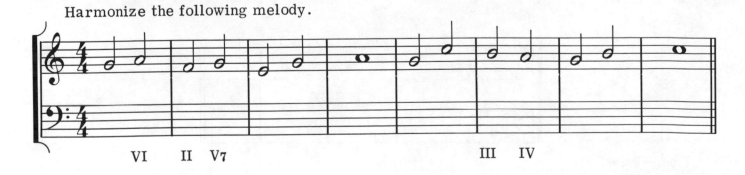

Fill in the two lower treble parts.

The Subdominant Triad is built on the fourth degree, IV, of the scale. It contains a root, major third, and perfect fifth. The chord ending IV to I is called the Plagal Cadence. When the root of the Tonic chord is in the top voice, it is called Perfect. If the third or fifth of the Tonic chord is in the top voice, it is called Imperfect.

A Perfect Plagal Cadence    An Imperfect Plagal Cadence

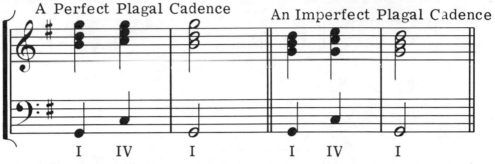

    I    IV    I        I    IV    I

Complete the following cadences and state whether they are Authentic (see page 47) or Plagal; Perfect or Imperfect.

The Subdominant Triad may progress to the Dominant or Dominant Seventh. When the third of any triad is in the bass, it is called a chord of the Sixth or a Six-Three chord because of the intervals it contains.

Harmonize the following melodies.

# AUGMENTED AND DIMINISHED TRIADS

An augmented triad is comprised of a major third and an augmented fifth.

Examples: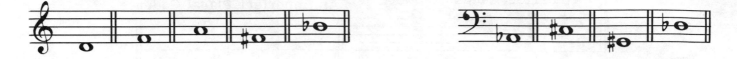

Construct augmented triads on the following notes:

A diminished triad is comprised of a minor third and a diminished fifth.

Examples: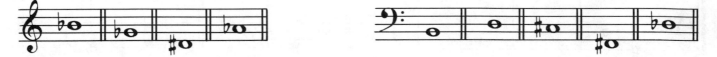

Construct diminished triads on the following notes:

Write a Major, minor, augmented, and diminished triad on each of the following notes.

# DOMINANT SEVENTH CHORDS
# (AND INVERSIONS)

If we add a minor seventh to the Dominant or V chord, it is then called the DOMINANT SEVENTH and is marked V7. The figure 7 may also be used after the letter name, (For example: C7; G7; D7-)

These are DOMINANT SEVENTH CHORDS

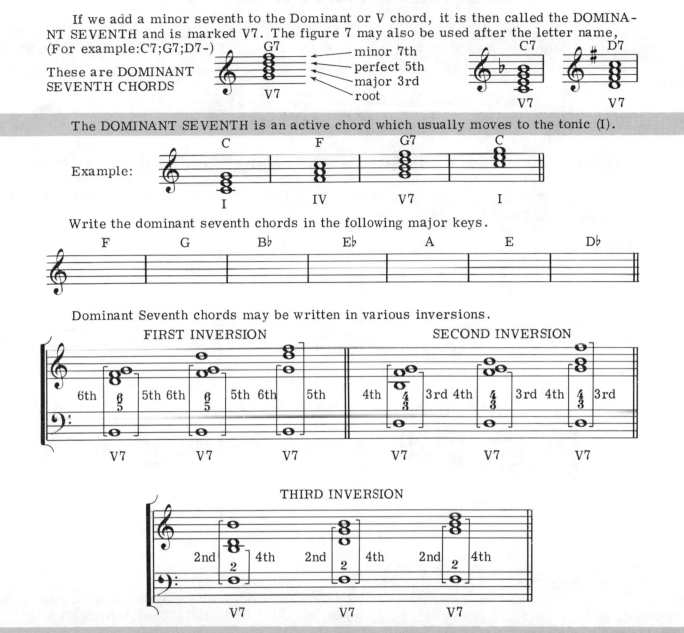

The DOMINANT SEVENTH is an active chord which usually moves to the tonic (I).

Example:

Write the dominant seventh chords in the following major keys.

F    G    Bb    Eb    A    E    Db

Dominant Seventh chords may be written in various inversions.

FIRST INVERSION        SECOND INVERSION

THIRD INVERSION

## FACTS ABOUT THE DOMINANT SEVENTH:

The root of the Dominant Seventh chord may be written in the bass, and is usually doubled in the upper voices. The Dominant triad very often precedes the Dominant Seventh. The Dominant Seventh may be repeated in a different position before resolving. Because of the minor seventh interval, the Dominant Seventh chord is more strongly attracted than the Dominant triad, towards the Tonic. It is used more often to precede the Tonic at the end of a phrase.

Harmonize the following melody.

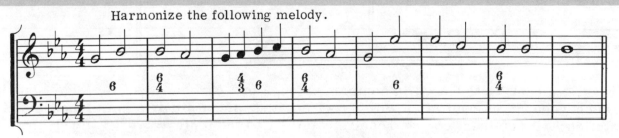

# THE MINOR SEVENTH AND DOMINANT NINTH CHORDS

The <u>Minor Seventh chord</u> is formed by adding the minor seventh interval to the minor triad. It is composed of a root, a minor third, a perfect fifth, and a minor seventh. The symbol is Am7 or Ami7.

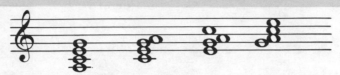

This chord contains both a major triad and its relative minor triad. In the <u>1st</u> inversion (Exp. 1), with the 3rd in the bass, it becomes major in quality. In the <u>2nd</u> and <u>3rd</u> inversions (Exp. 2 & 3) it is minor in quality as it is, of course, in its original position with the root in the bass (Exp. 4).

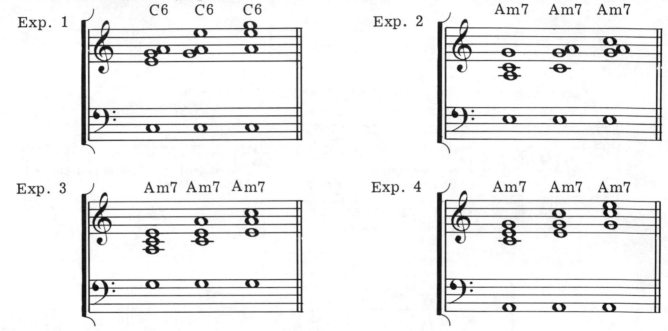

The <u>Dominant Ninth chord</u> is formed by adding the major ninth interval to the dominant seventh chord. It has the same inversions as the dominant seventh, and may be used instead. In four part harmony, the root, third or fifth is omitted. The ninth is usually found in the top voice, rarely the root.

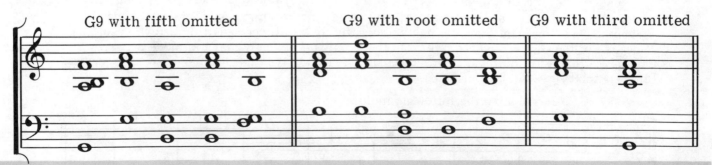

The Dominant Ninth Chord is sometimes found in a chromatic series. The discrimination between a dominant ninth with a root omitted, and a minor sixth, depends on the resolution. All dominant chords resolve naturally to the tonic.

# THE DIMINISHED SEVENTH AND AUGMENTED FIFTH CHORDS

The <u>Diminished</u> <u>Seventh</u> <u>chord</u> is composed of a root, a minor third, a diminished fifth and a diminished seventh. Example 1 is the correct notation of a Diminished Seventh on C.

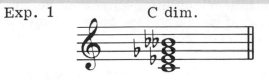

Because the correct notation is usually hard to read, "enharmonic equivalents" are used.

Enharmonically, there are only three of these chords. Therefore any note of the chord may be considered the root. The Diminished Seventh chord is usually distinguished by two accidentals. When using this chord, remember that each tone must resolve to the nearest tone of the next chord.

The <u>Augmented</u> <u>Fifth</u> <u>chord</u> is composed of a root, a major third and an augmented fifth. It resolves to the major or minor triad of which the root is the dominant. Enharmonically there are only four of these chords. Therefore any note of the chord could be the root. In four part harmony, the root is usually doubled, sometimes the third, but seldom the fifth. Study the following examples!

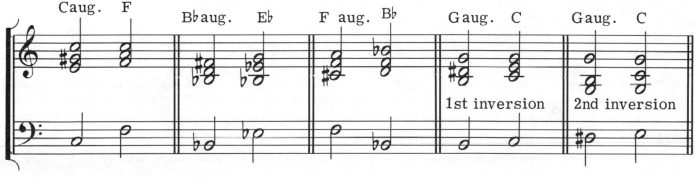

Harmonize the following melody.

53

# CHORD PROGRESSIONS AND PASSING TONES

Traditionally there have been several basic rules governing the progression of chords and chord sequences. To cover this area thoroughly one should use books that are totally devoted to harmony. In this particular book we will mention only the most common of the rules. Composition and harmonization of melodies takes much time and practice. The serious student should continue to work on his own, remembering that, except for certain fundamental principles, there are no hard and fast rules. There are pages of manuscript paper at the end of the book which may be used.

1. A chord may progress to another chord whose root is either a perfect fourth above or a perfect fifth below. In modern harmony, the VII chord is treated as a V7 chord, with the root missing.
   The progression of chord roots through the cycle of fifths is called Normal or Harmonic. This is often found in a series or sequential pattern.

Exp.

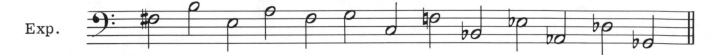

2. A chord may progress to another chord whose root is either a perfect fifth above or a perfect fourth below.

3. All major, minor or seventh chords built on degrees of a major scale are relative to its key.

4. A chord may progress to another chord whose root is either a major or minor third above or a major or minor third below.

5. An accidental in the melody sometimes indicates the third of a new chord. It is usually better to have contrary motion between the bass and melody. This sometimes calls for an inverted chord.

6. A chord may progress to another chord whose root is either a major or minor second above or a major or minor second below. When the root interval is a minor second, the chord progression is usually <u>chromatic</u>.

7. In harmonizing a melody, it should be kept in mind that one should finish with some form of the tonic chord.

## PASSING TONES

Many melodies contain notes which do not belong to the chords with which they sound. These are called passing tones (or non-harmonic tones). They either move too quickly to be harmonized separately or perhaps the composer simply does not wish to harmonize them in a chordal manner.

Example: ( ✗ = passing tone)

# FINAL REVIEW

1. Under the following notes write the letter name of the note.

2. Complete the time values in the following measures, using either notes or rests.

3. What notes are sharp in this key?

_____

4. What notes are flat in this key?

_____

5. Name the notes in the following exercise, (Note the key signature!)

E ___ ___ ___   ___ ___ ___   ___ ___ ___   ___

6. The interval between any two tones of a chromatic scale is a _____

7. Two or more notes differing in name but sounding the same pitch are called _____ tones.

8. Match the following signs with their correct definition:

   A - D.C.         _____ from the sign
   B - rit.          _____ gradually louder
   C - dim.        _____ coda sign
   D - ⊕           _____ gradually softer
   E - D.S.         _____ from the beginning
   F - cresc.     _____ gradually slower

9. Name the three relative minor scales: _____, _____, _____.

10. All minor scales begin on the _____ degree of their relative major scales.

11. Transpose the following melody from F Major to A Major.

# FINAL REVIEW-PART 2

12. Identify the following perfect and major intervals:

13. Using the I-IV-V chords harmonize the following melody and write the Roman numeral under each chord.

14. Write the progression I-IV-V7-I on the following staff:

        I        IV       V7        I

15. Harmonize the following bass passage.

16. Harmonize the following melodies.

17. Fill in the lower treble parts.

56

# CHROMATIC FINGERING CHART FOR GUITAR
## (LINES CONNECT IDENTICAL NOTES
## FOUND ON DIFFERENT STRINGS)

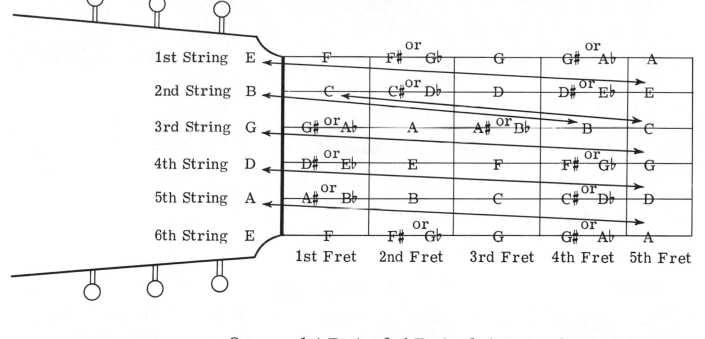

| | | 1st Fret | 2nd Fret | 3rd Fret | 4th Fret | 5th Fret |
|---|---|---|---|---|---|---|
| 1st String | E | F | F# or Gb | G | G# or Ab | A |
| 2nd String | B | C | C# or Db | D | D# or Eb | E |
| 3rd String | G | G# or Ab | A | A# or Bb | B | C |
| 4th String | D | D# or Eb | E | F | F# or Gb | G |
| 5th String | A | A# or Bb | B | C | C# or Db | D |
| 6th String | E | F | F# or Gb | G | G# or Ab | A |

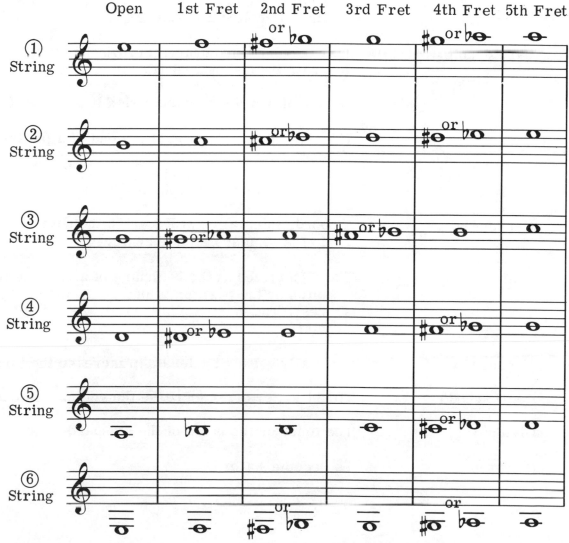

# DEFINITIONS OF COMMON MUSICAL TERMS

Accelerando — Gradually increasing the rate of speed.

Accent — Emphasis upon a certain note or beat.

Accidentals — All signs for raising or lowering the pitch that are not found in the key signature.

Adagio — To play slowly.

Allegro — To play at a high rate of speed though not so fast as presto.

Allegro con moto — Fast, with movement.

Allegro moderato — Moderately fast.

Andante — Play in moderate time.

Animato — Animated or lively.

Bar (bar line) — A line drawn through the staff to show the division of the time in a piece of music. The space between two bar lines is called a measure.

Bar, double — Heavy double lines drawn through the staff, usually to designate the end of a section or of a composition.

Beat — The regular underlying pulsation in a piece of music.

Cadence — The chordal progression at the end of a phrase, section or composition.

Chord — An organized vertical combination of musical sounds.

Chromatic — A chord, interval or scale which includes notes not belonging to the regular diatonic scale.

Clef — The sign placed at the beginning of a piece of music to fix the pitch or the position of one note, and consequently of the rest. The most common clefs are treble clef and bass clef.

Crescendo — Gradually getting louder or to increase the force of sound.

Decrescendo — To get softer or to decrease the volume of sound.

Diatonic — The tones or the notes of the standard major or minor scale.

Diminuendo — To become softer

| | |
|---|---|
| Dissonance | A discord |
| Dominant | The name applied to the fifth note of the scale. |
| Duple (double) | Two beats to the measure. |
| Dynamic | Refers to degrees of volume |
| Embellishment | The ornaments of melody (i.e., trill or turn) |
| Enharmonic | Having intervals less than a semitone |
| Fermata | Hold |
| Fine | The end. |
| Flat | Lowers the pitch of the note a semitone. |
| Frets | Small strips of wood, ivory or metal placed upon the fingerboard of certain stringed instruments (i.e., guitar or banjo). |
| Grandioso | Grand, noble |
| Harmony | The art of combining pitches or tones into chords. |
| Improvisation | "On the spur of the moment," an extemporaneous performance. |
| Interval | The difference in pitch between two tones. |
| Key | The series of tones forming any major or minor scale. |
| Largo | Very slowly. |
| Leading-note | The seventh degree of the ascending major scale |
| Ledger lines | The short additional lines drawn above or below the staff. |
| Legato | Smoothly and connected. |
| Maestoso | Majestically |
| Major scale | The scale which has semitones between the third and fourth and seventh and eighth degrees. |
| Marcato | To play with emphasis. |
| Measure | The portion of the music enclosed between two bar lines. |
| Melody | A succession of tones arranged rhythmically and symmetrically. |

| | |
|---|---|
| Minor scale | The scale formed by lowering the third and sixth degree of the major scale one-half step. |
| Modulation | The movement from one key to another by an organized succession of chords. |
| Natural | The character used to cancel a sharp or a flat. |
| Notation | In general, any musical sign (i.e., the staff, clef, notes, or rests) |
| Octave | Eight notes above or below the interval of an eighth. |
| Passing note | A melodic note, not essential to the chordal harmony. |
| Pitch | The heighth or depth of a tone expressed in number or vibrations per second. |
| Poco a poco | Little by little |
| Presto | Rapidly |
| Rallentando | Gradually getting slower |
| Repeat | A sign which indicates that certain measures or sections are to be performed twice. |
| Rests | Signs which indicate silence. |
| Rhythm | The organized arrangement of sound and silence. |
| Scale | A series of consecutive tones proceeding by half steps (chromatic) or by half steps and whole steps (major or minor) |
| Sharp | The sign which raises the pitch of a note one half step. |
| Signature | The sign such as sharps and flats placed at the beginning of a piece of music to show the key. |
| Slur | A curved line placed over notes directing that they be played legato. |
| Sostenuto | To sustain the tone |
| Staccato | To play in a crisp and detached manner. |
| Stem | The line attached to a note-head |
| Subito | Suddenly |

| | |
|---|---|
| Syncopation | To accent a normally unaccented beat, or to shift the accent from a strong beat to a weak beat. |
| Tablature | A system of notation used for certain stringed instruments (i.e., guitar or banjo) |
| Tempo | Rate of movement or speed of music |
| Tie | A curved line joining two notes of the same pitch and adding the duration of the second note to the first. |
| Transpose | To perform or to write a composition in a different key. |
| Triad | The common chord of three notes |
| Tuning | The adjustment of an instrument to a recognized pitch. |
| Unison | Pitches having the same number of vibrations per second. |
| Vivace | Lively. |

# Chord Chart

| Root | Major | Minor | Augmented | Diminished | Major 6 | Major 7 | Major 9 |
|---|---|---|---|---|---|---|---|
| C | C | Cm | C+ | C° | C6 | Cmaj7 | Cmaj9 |
| F | F | Fm | F+ | F° | F6 | Fmaj7 | Fmaj9 |
| B♭ | B♭ | B♭m | B♭+ | B♭° | B♭6 | B♭maj7 | B♭maj9 |
| E♭ | E♭ | E♭m | E♭+ | E♭° | E♭6 | E♭maj7 | E♭maj9 |
| A♭ | A♭ | A♭m | A♭+ | A♭° | A♭6 | A♭maj7 | A♭maj9 |
| D♭ | D♭ | D♭m | D♭+ | D♭° | D♭6 | D♭maj7 | D♭maj9 |
| G♭ | G♭ | G♭m | G♭+ | G♭° | G♭6 | G♭maj7 | G♭maj9 |
| B | B | Bm | B+ | B° | B6 | Bmaj7 | Bmaj9 |
| E | E | Em | E+ | E° | E6 | Emaj7 | Emaj9 |
| A | A | Am | A+ | A° | A6 | Amaj7 | Amaj9 |
| D | D | Dm | D+ | D° | D6 | Dmaj7 | Dmaj9 |
| G | G | Gm | G+ | G° | G6 | Gmaj7 | Gmaj9 |

# Chord Chart

| Minor 6 | Minor 7 | Minor 9 | (Dominant) 7 | (Dominant) 9 | (Dominant) 11 | (Dominant) 13 | Dim. 7 |
|---|---|---|---|---|---|---|---|
| Cm6 | Cm7 | Cm9 | C7 | C9 | C11 | C13 | C°7 |
| Fm6 | Fm7 | Fm9 | F7 | F9 | F11 | F13 | F°7 |
| B♭m6 | B♭m7 | B♭m9 | B♭7 | B♭9 | B♭11 | B♭13 | B♭°7 |
| E♭m6 | E♭m7 | E♭m9 | E♭7 | E♭9 | E♭11 | E♭13 | E♭°7 |
| A♭m6 | A♭m7 | A♭m9 | A♭7 | A♭9 | A♭11 | A♭13 | A♭°7 |
| D♭m6 | D♭m7 | D♭m9 | D♭7 | D♭9 | D♭11 | D♭13 | D♭°7 |
| G♭m6 | G♭m7 | G♭m9 | G♭7 | G♭9 | G♭11 | G♭13 | G♭°7 |
| Bm6 | Bm7 | Bm9 | B7 | B9 | B11 | B13 | B°7 |
| Em6 | Em7 | Em9 | E7 | E9 | E11 | E13 | E°7 |
| Am6 | Am7 | Am9 | A7 | A9 | A11 | A13 | A°7 |
| Dm6 | Dm7 | Dm9 | D7 | D9 | D11 | D13 | D°7 |
| Gm6 | Gm7 | Gm9 | G7 | G9 | G11 | G13 | G°7 |

# PRACTICAL RANGES FOR INSTRUMENTS

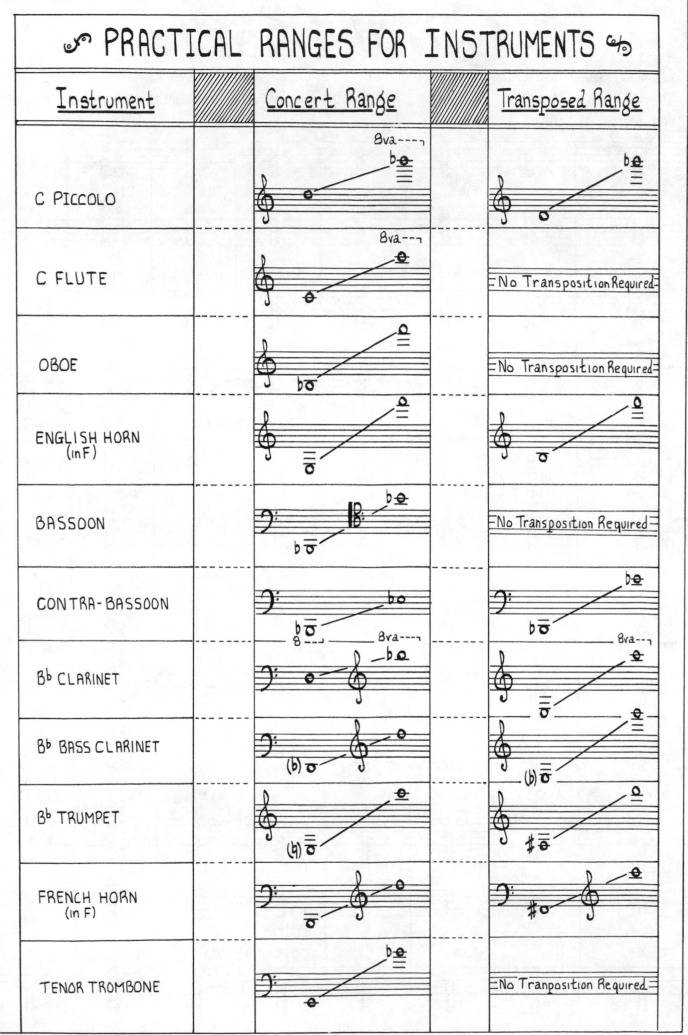

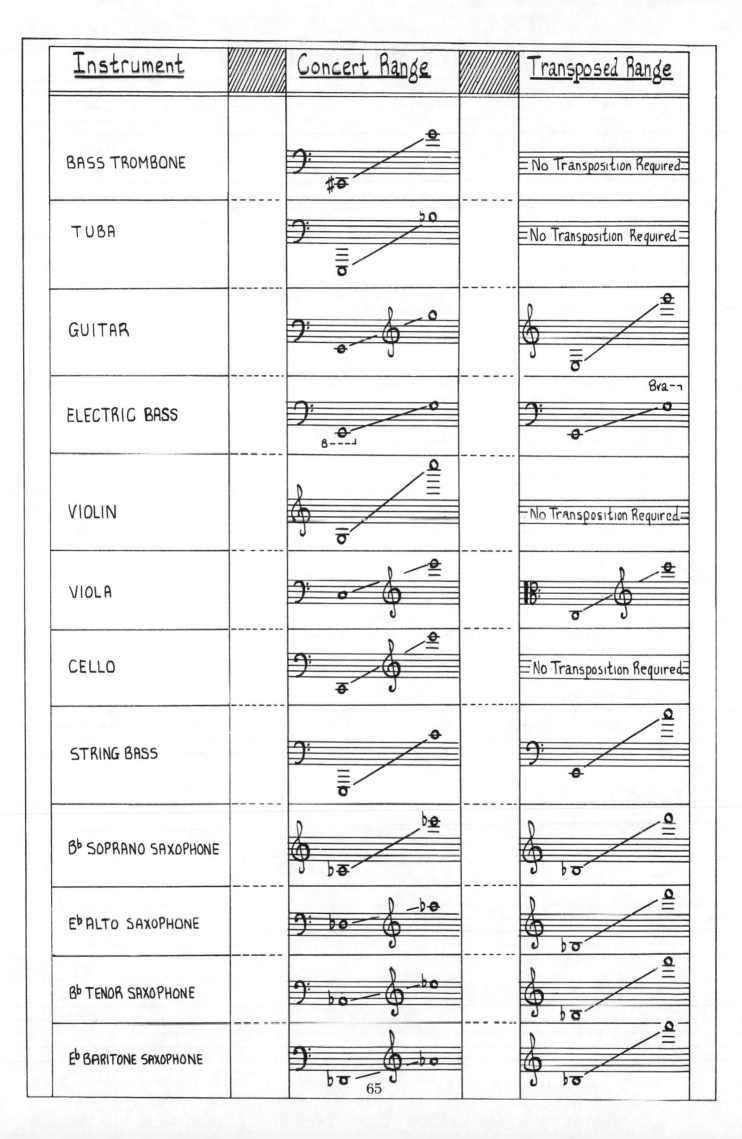

# THEORY WORKSHEET

# THEORY WORKSHEET

# THEORY WORKSHEET

# THEORY WORKSHEET
## (Keyboard)

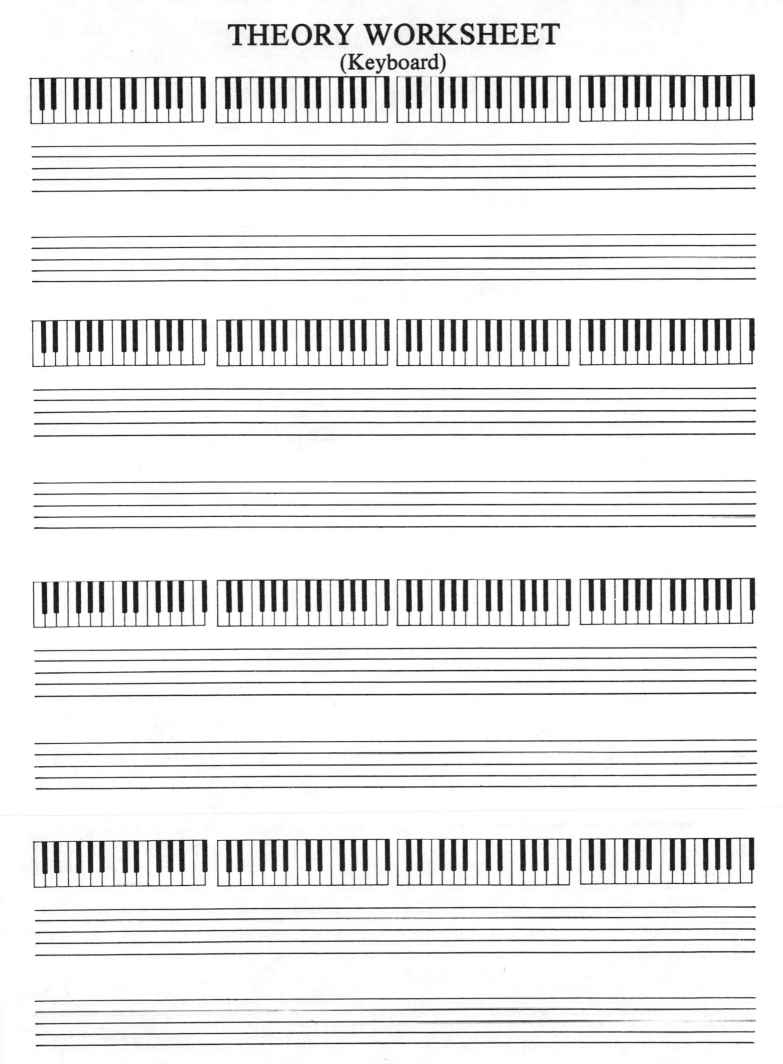

# THEORY WORKSHEET
## (Keyboard)

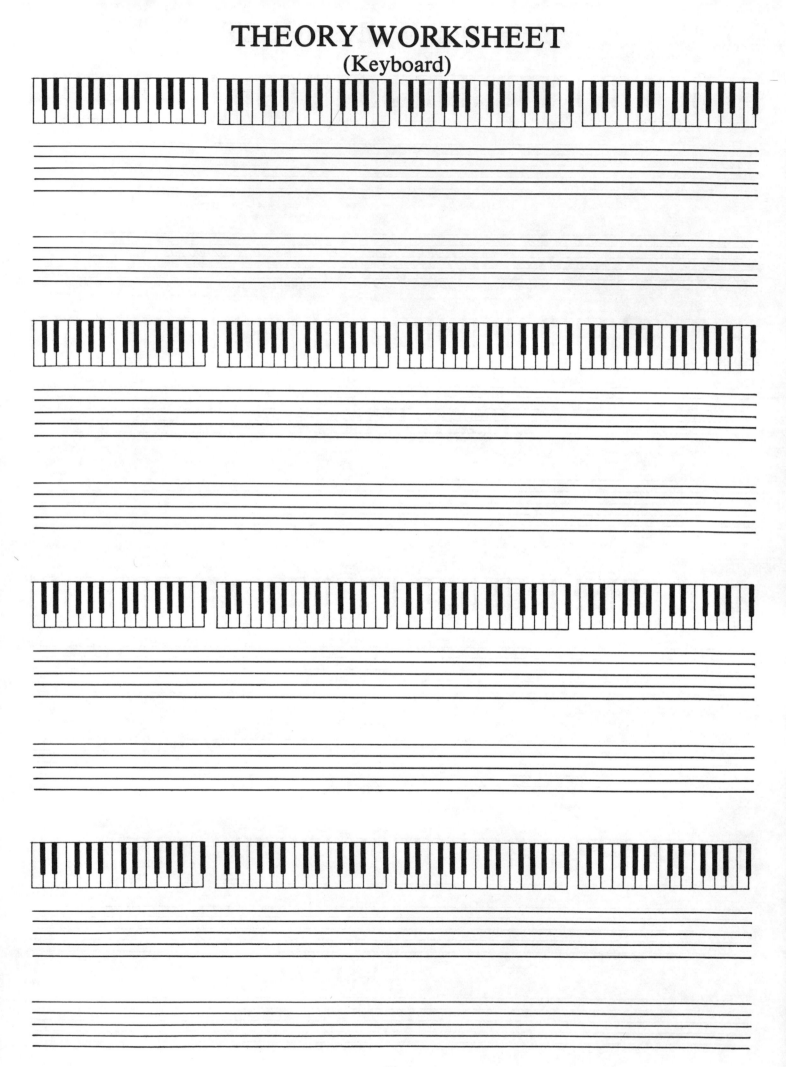

# THEORY WORKSHEET
## (Fretted Instruments)

# THEORY WORKSHEET
## (Fretted Instruments)

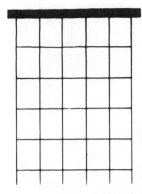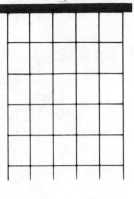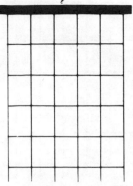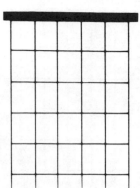

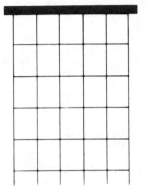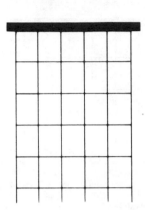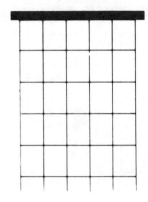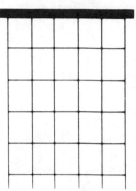

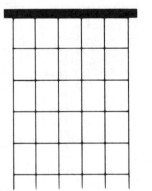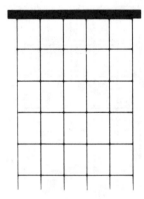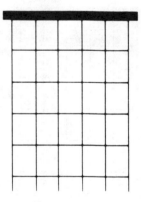